Harold Shipman

The True Story of Britain's Most Notorious Serial Killer

Ryan Green

ISBN-13: 978-1522788065
ISBN-10: 1522788069

CONTENTS

Introduction 6

Chapter 1 – Hiding just beneath the surface... 8

Chapter 2 – Discovery and Trial: Evil Unmasked 34

Chapter 3 – The Shipman Inquiry: Uncovering the Full Extent of His Crimes 57

Chapter 4 – Shipman's Motives and Motivation 82

Conclusion – Finding and Fixing the Oversights That Allowed Shipman to Kill 91

About the Author 96

HAROLD SHIPMAN

INTRODUCTION

The man on the cover of this book looks like he could be anyone's grandfather. It's easy to imagine him doting on his little grandkids, reading them stories from his lap and letting them play with his big, bushy beard. If you were told he was a doctor, I bet you'd imagine he was a good, kind and gentle one, with an easy, affable manner and deep care for his patients.

Harold Frederick Shipman certainly projected all those qualities, but only so that he could hide the evil that lurked deep inside. Shipman abused his trust and used his position to kill – no less than 218 of his patients found their end at his hand, making him the United Kingdom's most prolific serial killer by a long shot.

This book tells Shipman's story, from his childhood under a domineering mother to his pathetic death in a prison cell. It will put you in the perspective of those who lived and worked in proximity to him, showing you the considerate but sometimes haughty doctor he presented himself as before taking you through the process of wrenching off that mask and uncovering the full extent of the evil festering within.

We will make a study of the man's possible motives and close with a look at the systemic failures that allowed him to kill and steps taken to make sure nothing like his murderous spree ever happens again.

amazon Gift Receipt

Send a Thank You
Note

You can learn more about your gift
or start a return here too.

Scan using the Amazon app or visit
http://a.co/9awzVPS

**Harold Shipman: The True Story of Britain's Most
Notorious Serial Killer**

Order ID: 110-8294612-1423402   Ordered on December

A gift for you

HAPPY CHANUKAH! 5/7

Turn the page and begin to look into the life and mind of the ultimate human paradox: the healer who kills – '**Doctor Death**'.

CHAPTER 1 – HIDING JUST BENEATH THE SURFACE...

Knowing what we do today about everything that happened and what Shipman did, it's sometimes possible to forget the fact that those who lived and worked with him would have had a very different perception of him while they were living through it. Hindsight colours how we view the past and it is a lot easier for us to see warning signs and obvious red flags that we really might not have been able to connect if we were in the same situation as Harold Shipman's contemporaries.

There is no doubt that those red flags were there and that if someone had had the notion to diligently investigate and follow where they led, Shipman's killing spree would have been ended far sooner and a lot of grief and loss would have been avoided. We will examine some of them as we explore the story of Shipman's life before his crimes came to light in this chapter, but even as we do so, spare some effort to trying to put yourself in the place of Shipman's contemporaries and close relations. Try to forget the killer you know for a few moments and imagine how you would have reacted to the information available to you, and also remember that you might not have had any knowledge of even some of those surface facts that might have tipped the balance of suspicion for you.

Devils like Shipman deserve no sympathy, and this is by no means a plea to show him any. However, a really important part of figuring out how things like this can happen and of making sure they don't happen again that is often overlooked is gaining an understanding of the processes that were at play the minds of those who were living through the tragedy and yet were unable to see it. You can never predict it – any one of us can find ourselves in a similar situation someday, and we all need to be able to identify those thought processes that may blind us to what is happening.

Shipman's childhood

TV shows and books in the True Crime genre sometimes have a tendency to be overzealous in analysing the childhoods of killers and violent criminals to find connections between their upbringing and their actions to the point where they draw links far too tenuous to be taken seriously. The case of Harold Shipman is not one of those cases. This is one of those stories about which we can almost be completely certain that the way he was raised and the experiences he had in his younger years definitely informed and affected what happened later on.

Harold Frederick Shipman was born on the 14th of January 1946 to Vera and Harold Sr. He was their second child – "Freddy", as he was affectionately known, had a sister seven years older named Pauline and was joined by a younger brother named Clive four years after he was born. Despite his being in a normally less than privileged position among his siblings, Vera had a very special liking for Freddy. It was obvious even to neighbours that he was her favourite, and that she saw him as being the brightest and most promising of her offspring.

Vera had something of a superiority complex when it came to all of her children. She controlled who they could play with and when, but with her Freddy she took it to another level – where his brother and sister could dress casually he would have to wear a tie, and his associations were even more tightly controlled. That sense of superiority inevitably rubbed off on her son, and he grew up somewhat of a loner with few friends, though he was an enthusiastic athlete and played soccer in school.

The sequence of events that undoubtedly had the biggest impact on Harold Shipman's life was the illness and death of his mother. Sometime in his adolescence Vera developed terminal lung cancer, and the young Harold took it upon himself to be at her side and take care of her as much as he could. For him, this meant rushing straight home from school to be by her side and keep her company. Vera no doubt loved these sessions and grew to anticipate her Freddy coming home as the highlight of her day. Without a doubt, it's while spending time with his mother that Shipman developed the winning bedside manner that endeared his patients to him in his medical career.

Another thing he witnessed that would have altogether darker imprints on the future is that Shipman was also present when the family doctor was attending to Vera. This meant he was present when Vera's cancer was severely advanced and she was in constant pain. The doctor would administer morphine to Vera, and Shipman witnessed how her pain would instantly disappear almost as soon as the drug was administered. The fascination with opiates similar to morphine would never wane, and would manifest itself first as an object of personal addiction, and later as his chosen modus operandi for ending his victims' lives.

In a more general sense, it is almost certain that this proximity to someone so close to him in the last stages of her life, coupled with the almost angelic aspect he witnessed a medical professional in of taking away his mother's pain spurred him on to choose to become a doctor in the first place.

Vera passed away on June 21st 1963 and Harold would later bend all of his efforts towards entering the medical profession.

Primrose

A young man with a life as sheltered and with as little interaction with his peers as Harold Shipman had could reasonably have been expected to have very little luck with romance. Shipman, however, was more fortunate – he caught the eye of a young lady by the name of Primrose. Primrose had grown up in very similar conditions to Shipman – she too had a controlling mother who limited her interactions with other children, no doubt one of the factors that drew the two together.

In 1966, Shipman and Primrose got married – he at the age of 19, she at 17 and five months pregnant with their first child. Shipman beat the odds again with this whirlwind romance – the pair of them proved to be exceptionally well-matched for each other and remained together for the rest of his life. Primrose would stand by him through everything that happened and would vociferously come to his defence through a minor crisis early on in his career, as well as later on when his killing spree was uncovered.

Medical school

1965 was also the year Shipman got accepted into medical school. This was not on his first try – while Shipman had been a brilliant student during his earliest school days, he became mediocre at best as his education advanced and he had failed the entrance test the first time around. What he lacked in sheer brilliance, however, he made up for in a plodding determination that could not be dissuaded from a path once he had set his mind to it.

There is no doubt that Shipman was absolutely resolute in his desire to become a doctor. Who knows what the source of that determination was – perhaps at this stage all he had was just the desire to help people in the same way as he had seen his mother being helped. Or, perhaps, he already had the seeds of what would later happen germinating in his mind, and reaping a harvest of death was his intention all along. Whatever the case was, Shipman re-sat the entrance test and was successfully accepted into the University of Leeds medical program in September of 1965.

Shipman's time in medical school was little different from his later youth. He tackled his studies with the same lack of outright brilliance, but tempered by the sheer will to press on and do what he needed to do to get through. He was also just as reserved as he had been, with his peers noticing the same tendency towards haughtiness and aloofness instilled by his mother. The soccer field continued to be the one place where that fell away and he became an enthusiastic and very capable team player.

In June of 1970, at the age of 24, he graduated from medical school and was ready to begin his career.

Early career

Soon after leaving medical school, Shipman began his tenure as a house officer – a kind of post-medical school, pre-doctor position, what we more commonly call Residency – at the Pontefract General Infirmary in West Riding in the county of Yorkshire. His time there went without any outward incidents, and after 12 months Shipman was fully registered as a doctor with the General Medical Council, the board that certifies medical professionals in the UK. He thereafter spent another three years as a senior house officer at the same facility, also attaining a diploma in child health in 1972 and another diploma in obstetrics and gynaecology in 1974.

In early 1974 Shipman answered an ad in a medical publication and secured a position at the Abraham Ormerod Medical Centre in West Yorkshire. He had been taken on to replace a former partner at the practice who had retired on grounds of ill health. After a brief probationary period as an assistant general practitioner he became a junior partner.

Shipman was seen as an asset for the practice especially for his being relatively fresh out of medical school – he was much more up to date on the latest information and procedures compared to his veteran colleagues. If only all careers had that attitude. Shipman made good on this expectation, in particular pushing for an update of the practice's record-keeping systems.

Shipman also underwent a massive shift in his social character and the perception with which he was held, at least by his colleagues. Gone was the reclusive loner, and in his place was an outgoing, well-respected professional and member of the community. While he was respectful and genial with other doctors, the nurses and staff knew the old, bad side of Shipman. He was abrasive and confrontational, especially when someone was suggesting that things be done a different way from his own – he would demean and put down anyone who did that, often outright calling them stupid.

It's obvious that Shipman hadn't really changed deep inside. His sense of superiority was still there – he just didn't lord it over those who he saw as his equals, while those who were "beneath" him bore the brunt of it.

The pethidine chronicles

Shipman attacked his duties with enthusiasm, spearheading and doing much of the work needed to complete the records system upgrade. Another duty he took upon himself was the disposal of expired drugs and occasionally restocking the practice's supply. This being a very necessary task in the medical profession, and Shipman also having no prior record of mischief involving drugs, no one really saw any cause for concern.

The first suspicions of something untoward going on were raised by the Home Office Drugs Inspectorate, an arm of the government of the United Kingdom, and the West Yorkshire Police Drugs Squad in February of 1975. Shipman had been acquiring unusually large amounts of the drug pethidine, a synthetic opiate similar in action to the drug that was used to relieve his mother's pain, morphine. For much of the 20th century, pethidine was the most prescribed drug for the treatment of acute pain. Opiates are well-known for their highly addictive nature and the worry that Shipman was diverting excess quantities of the drug, whether for illicit sale or to feed a personal habit was very real.

The investigation into this didn't go very far – the investigating officers went no further than enquiring with the pharmacists supplying the drugs to Shipman. The pharmacists knew Shipman's good side – to them he was an absolute paragon of what a medical professional should be – "efficient and confident", in the exact words they used. They reassured the officers that Shipman was of absolutely upstanding character, and the investigation concluded that there was nothing to be worried about, though a watch would continue to be maintained in case anything else came to light.

This episode reveals a new, dark possibility around Shipman's change of outward bearing towards his colleagues. It could be that it was all a very deliberate façade, one specifically calculated to throw off any suspicions falling upon his behaviour. If this was indeed the case, then he was eminently successful on this one occasion and would benefit from it in hiding his much darker activities as well.

Drug abuse is a very difficult thing to hide, however, and cracks would soon begin to show in Shipman's own behaviour. Sometime in May of 1975, Primrose called in one of her husband's partner doctors after he had suffered a "blackout" in the bathroom, fallen and hit his head on the sink. Such episodes happened on several other occasions, and Shipman was referred to another doctor who diagnosed him with "idiopathic" epilepsy, meaning epilepsy for which the cause could not be identified. At Shipman's own initiative, he also decided to stop driving so as to prevent the risk of an accident if he suffered a "seizure", and relied on Primrose to drive him to the practice and to house calls.

Meanwhile, suspicion over the amounts of pethidine that were being acquired by Shipman was rising again. One supplier in particular was noticed to be supplying abnormally large quantities of the drug on orders and prescriptions submitted by him. The Home Office and police finally decided to interview Shipman himself and did so in June of 1975. Shipman was ready with his explanations for his acquiring of the drugs and assured the officers that nothing unseemly was happening with them.

The officials also checked with the practice for any possible evidence, but they hit a brick wall there: Shipman's documentation of controlled drugs was found to be lacking in several aspects, particularly the register of the number of times he administered pethidine to patients, even though this was required by the law. Some ampoules of intravenous pethidine acquired by Shipman were unable to be accounted for, but without the register it was impossible to confirm this.

All that resulted from this inquiry was a visit to the practice by a drugs inspector from the Home Office who delivered advice on maintaining a complete register of controlled drugs and also on the correct procedure for disposing of them.

It was probably this measure, as well as the alarm of receiving such an ominous official visit that led the practice to the discovery in September of 1975 that Shipman was indeed abusing pethidine and using his powers and responsibility to procure it. Shipman was called into a meeting by the other partners of the firm and confronted with the evidence. His initial reaction was to confirm the truth of this, and then try to use some of his charm and the camaraderie he had built up with his colleagues to persuade them to actually help him hide his addiction and continue to feed it with more illegal procurements of the drug.

The gall of this move is absolutely jaw dropping, and it isn't surprising at all that the partners rejected this proposal. And so denied, Shipman revealed his true nature and launched on a tirade, tending his resignation and then withdrawing it and telling the partners that they would have to force him out before storming out. Not long after, Primrose would show for the first time how fiercely she would defend her husband and stormed into the practice herself, repeating Shipman's assertion that he would not go willingly.

After taking legal advice, the practice managed to do just what Shipman had said they would have to and ejected him from the practice. They also notified the authorities of what had transpired, and on the 28th of November 1975 the police interviewed Shipman, now with the certain knowledge of his drug abuse.

Shipman had been checked into The Retreat, a drug rehabilitation centre, immediately after his expulsion from the practice and it is here that the police interviewed him. He denied any wrongdoing at first, but decided instead to come clean, telling the police what he professed to be the full extent of his wrongdoing. He told them that he had started taking pethidine around May of the year before to combat depression brought on by his being unable to get along with his partners in the practice. This, of course, came as a huge surprise to Shipman's erstwhile partners – when they read about the whole affair in the papers afterward because they weren't even aware Shipman had been subjected to a criminal investigation and trial while it was happening – who had known nothing but fruitful, cordial cooperation with him throughout their time working together.

The detective who interviewed Shipman, Detective Sergeant George McKeating noticed that all of Shipman's veins had collapsed – an effect that could only be the result of no less than five years' continuous use of intravenous drugs. It's most likely that Shipman had been abusing pethidine long before he joined the practice, possibly since the very beginning of his days as a house officer. This line of inquiry was not diligently pursued.

Shipman wrote a statement for the police detailing his addiction and the ways in which he had acquired the drugs. He also stated his intention never to return to practice as a general practitioner or to work in any position in which he would have access to pethidine.

Shipman cleaned up and was discharged from The Retreat on the 30th of December with a recommendation that he continue receiving psychiatric supervision for a few years. His "seizures" completely stopped not long after and by March of 1976 he began to drive himself around. It is obvious with hindsight that his abuse of pethidine was their cause.

On February the 13th of 1976, Shipman was brought to the Halifax Magistrates' Court and presented with three charges of obtaining ten ampoules of 100 milligram pethidine by deception, three charges of illegal possession of pethidine and one charge of forging a prescription (his principal way of obtaining the drug) and plead guilty to all of them. He was convicted but didn't receive ant prison time or heavy censure, instead being slapped with a £75 fine for each one, for a total of £600.

Even while criminal proceedings were being brought against him, Shipman was moving on with his career. On February the 2nd 1976, he started work at the Newton Aycliffe Health Centre, administered by the Durham Area Medical Authority, as a clinical medical officer. He was upfront with his employers about the legal trouble he was going through. They consulted with the psychiatrists he had been receiving treatment from and on their advice offered him the job on the condition that he continue receiving treatment. The position didn't violate the terms of trust he had set for himself as he didn't have any access to controlled drugs.

The details of Shipman's convictions were reported to the General Medical Council and were brought before its Penal Cases Committee, the branch responsible for assessing criminal cases being faced by GMC members and deciding whether they should be brought before the Disciplinary Committee. The PCC took advice from the doctors Bryce and Milne, the psychiatrists who had been treating Shipman, and they also took into account a letter of support from his employer at the Durham Area Medical Authority stating that he was settling in well in his new job and was showing no signs of being in danger of relapsing.

With this in mind, the PCC decided it wasn't necessary to take any disciplinary action on Shipman. They did send a strongly worded letter that expressed in no uncertain terms that if Shipman was convicted of any similar drug-related offences he would face the full brunt of a disciplinary enquiry.

This decision meant that in the GMC's eyes, Shipman was free to continue practicing as a doctor, but there was still an avenue that could bar him from doing so. Under the Misuse of Drugs act, the office of the Home Secretary had the power to bar Shipman from his profession and from any position whatsoever in which he would have access to controlled drugs. The choice to do so was not made, and the GMC's own decision not to expel Shipman was probably a factor in this.

Another factor in that decision was the view given by the police that Shipman's patients had not suffered from his actions. This decision in particular might have been painfully ironic because it later on came out that Shipman could already have begun killing his patients. It is certain that he did kill afterwards, and his choice of lethal instrument was the very controlled substances he would have been banned from ever obtaining. Had that happened it is certain that hundreds of lives would have been spared.

Continuing career

Shipman held his position with the Durham Area Medical Authority for a while and also took up a temporary position with the National Coal Board. With no barriers to his re-entering full practice as a doctor, though, it was only a matter of time before he returned. In 1977, he answered an ad for a GP position at the Donneybrook practice in Hyde, a town now a part of the Greater Manchester metropolitan area.

Shipman told the partners at the practice all about his trouble with pethidine and the resultant convictions and referred them to one of the psychiatrists who treated him. After consulting with the psychiatrist, as well as the GMC and the Home office, the partners offered Shipman a position at the practice based on the assurances they had received that Shipman was not undergoing any current trouble with drug abuse or his mental health, and that he was under no restrictions that would prevent him from handling and administering controlled drugs. On the first of October 1977, Shipman began working at the Donneybrook practice.

Donneybrook was the longest stage of Shipman's career, and he presented himself in much the same way as he had in his previous GP position in Todmorden. He was an innovator who championed the introduction of new ways of doing things and was heavily involved in other organizations outside of the practice. Some positions he held include area surgeon for the local St John Ambulance, a membership with the Local Practitioners committee and a secretary position with the Tameside Local Medical Committee.

He was also way ahead of his time when it came to preventative medicine – he was recommending regular health check-ups regardless of how the patient was feeling long before it became a regular thing.

The dedication Shipman showed to his patients was exemplary – morning appointments were commonly slated to last seven minutes each but he would spend more time than necessary with each patient, the excess spent just chatting with them about events and their lives. His allotted morning surgery time would often overrun by thirty minutes, sometimes more. While his partners were taking lunch, Shipman would be beginning his home visitation rounds. Many of these were unannounced, non-appointment visits to check in on the patients and he continued doing this long after it stopped being a common thing for doctors to do as the population grew and more demands were placed on their time.

His interpersonal relationships were a little different, though. He was still the absolute epitome of what a doctor should be to his patients and was as a result extremely well loved by them, but with his colleagues he was a little less magnanimous. His individualism and insistence on things being done his way would assert themselves more and more as time went on, to the point where relations with other partners would begin to deteriorate.

In 1991, Shipman told his partners of his intention to leave the practice. He gave two reasons for this: one was that he disliked the computer system that had been introduced in the practice in 1989. The other was his disagreement with the way the other partners were proposing they institute the system of fundholding. Fundholding was a controversial initiative by the UK National Health Service for allowing general practices to set their own budgets with government allocated money.

The former reason makes little sense in the light of Shipman's established reputation as an innovator, and it seems especially spurious once we take later events into consideration – once Shipman had established his own practice he enthusiastically embraced computerized record keeping, even becoming head of the local user group for a software system especially developed for doctors known as Micro-Doc.

In a similar vein, Shipman also took to Fundholding with gusto after forming his own practice, joining the Tameside Consortium (South), a fundholding group for local doctors. Shipman's conversations over the issue with his partners definitely made it seem like he was against the concept of fundholding but when he was questioned about it during his trial he gave as a reason that he believed his partners were not as committed to fundholding as he was.

In hindsight, these reasons seem to have been misdirection on Shipman's part. When his partners at the Donneybrook practice were questioned, they seemed to find it likely that his real reason was a desire to branch off into single practice because of his individualistic approach to medicine, as well as his sometimes acrimonious relations with his partners. This is notable as an inversion of his previous justifications for his pethidine use – back then he fabricated hostility with his partners that they themselves denied while this time he diverted attention away from the friction between him and his partners while they confirmed it.

The darkest but also very much likely possibility is that Shipman was finding it difficult to continue his patient-killing activities and hide them at the same time while in a shared practice. Going off on his own would give him the freedom to continue unhindered and without such a high risk of detection.

On the January 1st 1992 Shipman began practicing privately while still within Donneybrook House and preparing his private surgery. In August of the same year he moved into his new premises at 21 Market Street in Hyde, taking with him some staff from Donneybrook and his patient list. The parting was quite acrimonious and had to involve a lot of legal wrangling over the financial arrangements caused by Shipman's leaving. The biggest source of discord was Shipman's taking of his patient list – while Donneybrook was a shared practice each doctor had their own list of patients and only treated each other's patients when the doctor in question was out or otherwise occupied. Shipman, in part due to his extreme popularity with patients had the largest patient list among his partners, a source of revenue the drying up of which would see the practice take a particularly hard financial knock.

Once he went into single practice, Shipman's reputation soared. He was especially popular among elderly patients, in part for his willingness to make home visits to them. Much of his fame spread by word of mouth, and a lot of patients clamoured to be on his list because of recommendations given by family and friends that were already receiving care from him and were massively impressed by his charm and the seemingly deep care he exhibited toward his patients. He wound up actually having so many patients he couldn't fit new ones onto his list. The joy at being accepted to be one of Shipman's patients was, in the words of one such fortunate, on par with having "won the lottery". By the time he was arrested, Shipman was in the process of trying to bring in a partner to try to relieve his workload.

Another area in which he excelled was in instituting rigorous audit practices, to the point where he was held in such high esteem by the Health Authority's Audit Group as to be the go-to name that was brought up when inquiries into audit practices that needed the input of a general practitioner were being made. He was also active in local medical politics and became a treasurer of the local branch of the Small Practices Association.

All of these factors contributed to Shipman being widely regarded as the "best doctor in Hyde", as testified by the widower of one of his colleagues in the area. Shipman's murderous activities were beginning to rise to a pitch that could no longer be hidden or ignored, though, and very soon suspicions were going to be raised that would lead to the unravelling of the web that had kept them out of view. His community and the world would soon receive the appalling true picture of just the kind of doctor Harold Shipman was.

The first suspicions are raised

As part of his strategy for hiding his crimes, Shipman would instruct the families of his patients that cremation was the best option for laying their family member to rest. Anyone familiar with forensics knows how false the adage "dead men tell no tales" is – a dead body, even at highly advanced stages of decomposition, can tell plenty about how its owner died. Ashes, on the other hand, cannot. In particular, the extreme heat of cremation destroys large, complex organic molecules – molecules like opiates, for example. Not knowing the true diabolical reasons for Shipman's insistence, a very large number of them took the genial, seemingly trustworthy doctor's advice.

The finality of cremation in terms of finding out anything meaningful about a deceased person's demise from their remains was well-recognized, and a series of measures was built around the process of certifying a body for cremation that aimed to make sure that there was no suspicion of foul play or anything untoward in their death. The first was a form – Form B – to be filled out by a doctor who had taken care of the deceased before their death and had identified the body – in every case Shipman himself. The doctor was supposed to give certain details about the patient's medical history, the cause of death, who had been with the deceased at time of death, and also certify that they had identified the body. This was meant to establish whether the cause of death was consistent with their medical history and make sure there was nothing suspicious about the death itself. Shipman liked to play fast and loose with the facts, though, and since he was the doctor who also certified death and determined its cause, this measure didn't particularly trouble him at all. We'll take a deeper look at the extent of Shipman's fabrications and the shortcomings that allowed him to get away with them in later chapters.

Form C was the next form to be filled, and it was to be filled by a doctor from another practice. The said second doctor was supposed to carefully examine the body, question the doctor who had filled Form B to gather the deceased's medical history, and then certify that the deceased did not perish under any suspicious or violent circumstances. A fee of £45.50 was paid to the Form C doctor – a practice some have wryly called "cash-for-ash". There were shortcomings with this practice as well that caused the failure to identify Shipman's unlawful activities.

A third form, Form F, was then filled by a medical referee at the crematorium who checked over the two previous forms and gave the go-ahead to cremate the body of the deceased. At any point in this process, someone could raise the alarm if they noticed anything suspicious and demand a post-mortem examination, and even after that, so could the crematorium staff. And yet in all the years of Shipman murdering his patients, no one did.

It was the Form C measure that first raised suspicion, though. By necessity, Shipman had to make Form C requests to practices operating in the same vicinity of Hyde, and one of the practices he patronized for this service was the Brooke practice, right across the street from Shipman's own surgery. On March 24th 1998, just over four and a half years after establishing his premises on Market Street, Dr. Linda Reynolds, one of the partners of the Brooke practice raised concerns with the coroner for the Greater Manchester South District, Mr. John Pollard, about the number of Form Cs they were filling out for Shipman.

The Brooke practice was a multi-doctor practice and had a patient list about three times the size of Shipman's, and in the three months before Dr. Reynolds' report they had experienced fourteen patient deaths. Shipman had in the same period submitted sixteen Form C requests to the Brooke practice. Bear in mind that this figure was just patients of Shipman's that were cremated, and also only those for whom he submitted Form C requests to the Brooke practice. It did not include those that were buried, those who had died in hospital or had their deaths certified by the coroner (Shipman would have had no hand in processing those), or Form Cs that he would have submitted to other practices.

Dr. Reynolds did not at the time have specifics for these other figures but even a conservative estimate would have yielded a stupendous number. The other suspicious factor, reported to Dr. Reynolds by Mrs. Deborah Bambroffe, a partner and undertaker at Frank Massey and Sons, Funeral Directors, who often attended to the bodies of Shipman's deceased patients was the eerie similarity in the circumstances surrounding a very large number of Shipman's patients' deaths. A very large number of them were female, lived and were found alone, were often in good health, and Shipman himself was often present or "discovered" their deaths. They were also often fully clothed and seated peacefully when found, whereas it could be expected that a sudden, unexpected death would find the patient partially clothed or in bed and in their night clothes in more cases than were found, and would probably have fallen or had evidence of a brief struggle as they realized something wasn't right.

The coroner made a report to the Greater Manchester Police, particularly Chief Superintendent David Sykes and Detective Inspector David Smith. Detective Inspector Smith then undertook the investigation. From the details of the investigation that came out in Shipman's trial, it is obvious that DI Smith never took the charges seriously and did not fully understand the implications of what Dr. Reynolds was saying. He failed to ask several deeper, vital questions that would have clarified things during his interview of her and, perhaps most egregiously, when he was told that there were two bodies whose deaths were certified by Shipman that were in the morgue pending cremation, he did not request autopsies and toxicology analyses be performed on them.

Following the interview with Dr. Reynolds, DI Smith requested copies of the death certificates of deaths certified by Shipman within the six months preceding. Shipman had certified 31 deaths, but due to a clerical error at the registry office, Smith only received 20 copies. Because he didn't really understand the significance of the numbers given him by Dr. Reynolds he failed to realize that the number of certificates he received was far too low. As a result, he continued with the investigation with a gross underestimation of the true magnitude of what he was investigating.

DI Smith then made requests for the medical records of the twenty individuals to be examined. However, without the consent of the deceased's next-of-kin, he couldn't view the documents himself and had to have them assessed by Dr. Alan Banks, a medical adviser to the health authority. Dr. Banks was acquainted with Shipman, knew his reputation in the community and held him with the same respect many of his colleagues did. Without a serious outlook on the allegations himself, DI Smith was unable to communicate the gravity of the situation or the extent of the disparities in Shipman's death figures. It's possible that if Dr. Banks had had the full number of deaths certified by Shipman he would have found that quite alarming, but as it was, these factors led him not to take the allegations with much seriousness at all.

Of the twenty certified deaths, Dr. Banks was tasked with finding seventeen sets of medical records and was only able to get his hands on those of fourteen patients. Of those, thirteen were female – a stupendously unlikely statistic – and none of them had any serious conditions leading up to their deaths. Twelve of the patients also died in their own homes, with only two happening at nursing homes. Yet Dr. Banks did not find any of this odd or alarming, or if he did let his personal view of Shipman dispel his suspicions. He would dismiss "common features" on the basis that they were not uniform across all the deaths, an illogical decision to make. Overall, he appears to have undertaken his study of the records with the prejudgment that the allegations were absurd and unlikely, and that led to his reporting back to DI Smith that there was nothing to worry about and that only two of the fourteen records could, perhaps, maybe have warranted a deeper look into the causes of death.

Dr. Banks' testimony probably put the final nail in the coffin of the investigation as far as DI Smith was convinced in his own mind, but he made one more inquiry all the same. On April 1st 1998 he made a visit to the Dukenfield crematorium, the regional crematorium where all of Shipman's patients were cremated. He didn't really do much there – he failed to ask about the system of certification for cremations, as a result completely missing the Form B's Shipman had filled, as well as failing to ask to view the crematory's register, which would have revealed to him the 11 deaths he had missed and perhaps caused him to see things in their truer, more sinister light.

Never really having treated his investigation with the full gravity it deserved, on April 15th 1998 Detective Inspector Smith met with Chief Superintendent Sykes to deliver his finding that there was no evidence to point to Shipman having killed any of his patients. CS Sykes then gave him the permission to close the investigation as he saw fit. DI Smith did so without much ceremony, never even writing a report of the investigation. At no point were criminal records outside of the Greater Manchester Police's criminal records system, which would have revealed Shipman's previous convictions for drug offences, neither was he interviewed himself.

CHAPTER 2 – DISCOVERY AND TRIAL: EVIL UNMASKED

Through the actions of another person who held him in such high esteem that they thought the whole fiasco was not just absurd, but also an almost insulting affront to his character, Shipman became aware that he had been under investigation. Without a doubt this scared the white willies out of him, and for a short while he put a stop to his behind-the-scenes 'god play' with the lives of his patients.

We'll take a deeper look at what could possibly have motivated Shipman to do what he did in a later chapter, but whatever it is, it seems to have twisted his mind to the point where it either clouded his good sense and reason, or it had become so big of a compulsion that he was no longer in control of it (if he ever had been). A smarter, more cautious person would have ended their activities as soon as they heard that they had been under police investigation, no matter how shallow that investigation had been. After a hiatus Shipman, however, resumed his killing.

He could very well have continued doing so without detection indefinitely until someone raised alarm that could not be ignored as had happened during his earlier debacles over misappropriation and abuse of pethidine. What wound up being his downfall was his very odd introduction into one particular murder of a factor that had never been a part of his routine before.

On June 24th 1998 Kathleen Grundy, a patient of Shipman's died unexpectedly at the age of 81. She had been mentally and physically active, well capable of living on her own and taking care of herself – a perfect picture of health and vitality during the later years of life. And yet Shipman certified her death as having been due to "old age" – a tactic that, as we will see, had very successfully hidden his activities over the years and probably would have done the same in this case.

Mrs. Grundy had a daughter, Angela Woodruff, who was a practicing attorney. Mrs. Woodruff had always taken care of her mother's legal affairs, including her will, which had her as the sole beneficiary of Mrs. Grundy's estate. You can imagine her absolute surprise, then, when she received news that a new will had apparently been drawn up without her knowledge and delivered to another law firm.

The "new will" (Image source: The Shipman Inquiry, First Report)

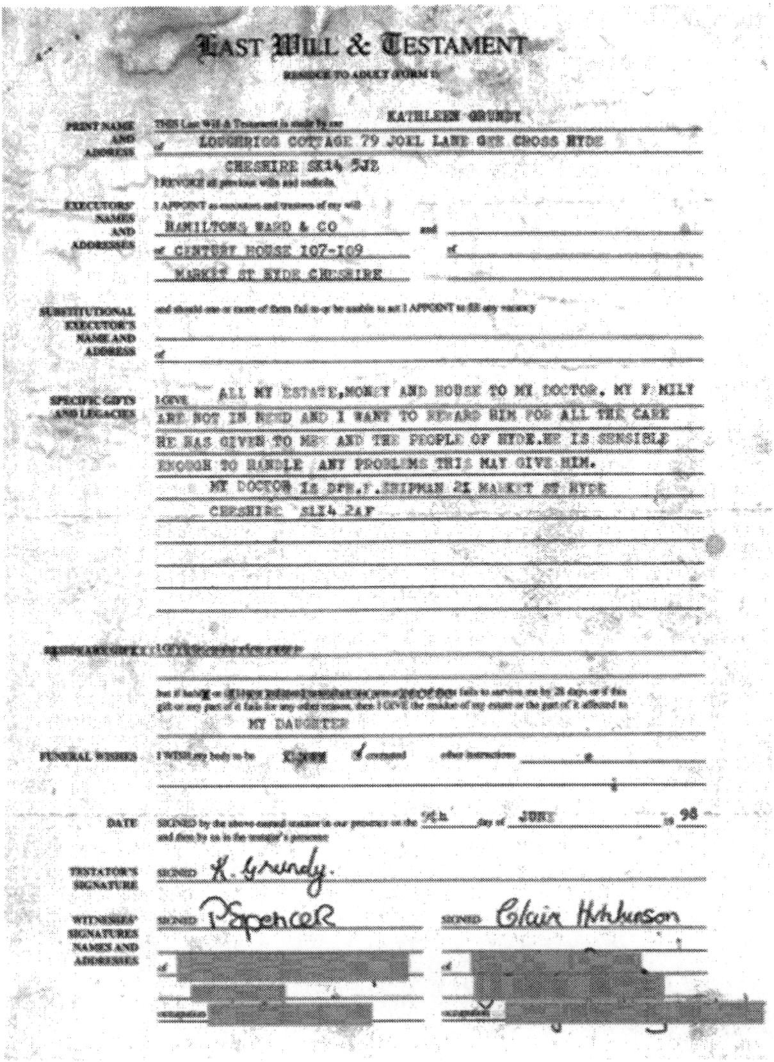

LAST WILL & TESTAMENT

PRINT NAME AND ADDRESS: This Last Will & Testament is made by me KATHLEEN GRUNDY of LOUGHRIGG COTTAGE 79 JOEL LANE GEE CROSS HYDE CHESHIRE SK14 5JE

I REVOKE all previous wills and codicils.

EXECUTORS' NAMES AND ADDRESSES: I APPOINT as executors and trustees of my will HAMILTONS WARD & CO and of CENTURY HOUSE 107-109 MARKET ST HYDE CHESHIRE of

SUBSTITUTIONAL EXECUTOR'S NAME AND ADDRESS: and should one or more of them fail to or be unable to act I APPOINT to fill any vacancy of

SPECIFIC GIFTS AND LEGACIES: I GIVE ALL MY ESTATE,MONEY AND HOUSE TO MY DOCTOR. MY FAMILY ARE NOT IN NEED AND I WANT TO REWARD HIM FOR ALL THE CARE HE HAS GIVEN TO ME AND THE PEOPLE OF HYDE.HE IS SENSIBLE ENOUGH TO HANDLE ANY PROBLEMS THIS MAY GIVE HIM.
MY DOCTOR IS DR.H.F.SHIPMAN 21 MARKET ST HYDE CHESHIRE SK14 2AF

RESIDUARY GIFT

but if he/she or ... fails to survive me by 28 days or if this gift or any part of it fails for any other reason, then I GIVE the residue of my estate or the part of it affected to MY DAUGHTER

FUNERAL WISHES: I WISH my body to be buried / cremated other instructions

DATE: SIGNED by the above-named testator in our presence on the 9th day of JUNE 19 98 and then by us in the testator's presence

TESTATOR'S SIGNATURE: SIGNED K. Grundy.

WITNESSES' SIGNATURES NAMES AND ADDRESSES: SIGNED P Spencer SIGNED Claire Hutchinson

of [redacted] occupation [redacted]

of [redacted] occupation [redacted]

The cover letter (Image source: The Shipman Inquiry, First Report)

KATHLEEN GRUNDY
LOUGHRIGG COTTAGE
79 JOEL LANE
HYDE
CE SHIRE
SK14 5JZ
22.6.98

RECEIVED 2 4 JUN 1998

Dear Sir,

I enclose a copy of my will. I think it is clear in intent. I wish Dr. shipman to benefit by having my estate but if he dies or cannot accept it ,then the estate goes to my daughter.

I would like you to be the executor of the will, I intend to make an appointment to discuss this and my will in the near future.

Yours sincerely

K. Grundy.

The letter from "J." or "S. Smith" (Image source: The Shipman Inquiry, First Report)

RECEIVED 3 0 JUN 1998

28 JUNE 1998

Dear Sir,

I regret to inform you that Mrs K. Grundy, of 79 Joel Lane Hyde . died last week.

I understand that she lodged a will with you, as I am a friend typed it out for her.

Her daughter is at the address and you can contact her there.

Yours

J. Smith,

The new will, drawn up on the 9th of June named Shipman as the sole benefactor of Mrs. Grundy's estate, and was accompanied by a cover letter purportedly signed by her. It noted that her family were "not in need" and she wanted to reward Shipman, "for all the care he has given to me and the people of Hyde". It was also apparently witnessed by two of Shipman's other patients. On the June 30th 1998, six days after Mrs. Grundy's death, the law firm the new will was lodged with received a letter from a person signing themselves as "J. Smith" or "S. Smith" informing them of her death.

Mrs. Woodruff was immediately, rightfully suspicious about the whole affair and took it upon herself to investigate the provenance of the will. It really did not take much for the validity of her suspicions to be confirmed – all it took was a visit to the two named witnesses on the new will. What she heard from them was so unsatisfying as to almost confirm her suspicions. On July 24th 1998, she made a report to the police in her home county of Warwickshire who passed it on to the Greater Manchester Police, who in turn immediately realized that the doctor on the will was the very same one they had investigated on suspicion of killing his patients just four months earlier.

A warrant to search Shipman's premises and home were executed on August 1st 1998, leading to the seizure of a typewriter and medical records. On the same day Mrs. Grundy's body was exhumed and a post-mortem exam took place. The initial exam was unable to establish the cause of death – meaning Shipman's attribution of it to old age was spurious. Toxicological tests were ordered and showed that an opiate was present in the body, though the exact type and levels were uncertain. More tests were needed to ascertain these.

On August the 1oth, the Greater Manchester police were informed by the Home Office Drugs Inspectorate about Shipman's past conviction over drugs offences. This was the first time the Manchester police came to know that he even had a previous criminal record. Shipman was questioned over this on the 14th. At some point, a re-examination of the 19 deaths certified by Shipman was ordered, as well as interviews of their families over whether they had any concerns about the circumstances surrounding the deaths, and a further nine deaths which were missed thanks to the clerical error at the registry office were later included.

The will documents were inspected by a forensic documents examiner on August the 26th. What the examination revealed was that Mrs. Grundy's signature on it were forgeries and that it was probably typed using the typewriter police had seized from Shipman's office. On the 28th investigators were told that the opiate found in Mrs. Grundy's body was morphine, and that the levels it had been found in had previously been known to cause death by overdose.

On September 7th 1998, Shipman was finally arrested on suspicion of causing the death of Mrs. Grundy, as well as for the forgery of the will. Over the course of the next few months the bodies of several patients

Shipman had certified the deaths of in the preceding two years who had been buried rather than cremated were exhumed, while the circumstances of several others which were cremated were thoroughly examined. He would be charged with the murder of fourteen more victims by the end of February 1999 – six of whose bodies had been cremated. None of the deceased had been prescribed morphine or any of its derivatives but all of the buried had traces of it in their bodies.

Shipman was interviewed with each batch of charges that came in. The first interview had to be discontinued after he became distressed and incoherent. Subsequent ones yielded from him nothing but a "no comment".

The police communicated to the General Medical Council the charges being brought against Shipman, but according to their own rules they were powerless to do anything until Shipman had actually been convicted of a crime. The West Pennine Health Authority passed the charges on to a body that did have the power to end Shipman's career, which was the National Health Service Tribunal. There were several long delays in the process – though the Health Authority had communicated with the Tribunal on August the 18th, it was only able to hold a hearing on September the 29th, deciding to suspend Shipman from practice. This decision was not communicated to the Health Authority until October 15th, and they were only able to seize his practice after a fourteen day appeal period had passed.

The Shipman Trial

The trial of Harold Shipman opened on the 5th of October 1999, and he was charged with the fifteen counts of murder and one of forgery. He pled not guilty to every single one of them. Shipman's defence counsel attempted to get the court to try him separately for the cases that had physical evidence, the cases that did not and the Grundy case, which was unique due to the fraud aspect, but the request was denied on account that this would take an inordinate amount of time and come at a prohibitive financial cost. Shipman's incarceration or freedom would stand on just this one shot.

The prosecution's arguments

The prosecution opened the case by alleging that Shipman killed his patients out of enjoyment and the thrill of exercising power over life and death. While this is a common motivation for serial killers and one which deserves a great deal of consideration, no psychiatric evaluation had ever been made of Shipman to support this notion, and since he was maintaining his innocence, no confession to back this could have come from him. Making this assertion in a court of law could really have come back to bite the prosecution's case in the rear end if the rest of the case they built had not been so compelling.

The toxicology reports from the post-mortem examinations performed on the exhumed bodies was the crux of the prosecution's case. Only one of the deceased had been prescribed morphine and there was no easy way to account for its presence in all of their systems except by the common thread of their having Shipman as their doctor and the proximity of their deaths with a visit from him.

Shipman was occasionally seen leaving the patients' homes by neighbours. In the case of Jean Lilley who was aged 59, her neighbour Elizabeth Hunter saw him leave her house and went in to visit straight after. She found Mrs. Turner blue in the lips and not breathing and unsuccessfully attempted mouth-to-mouth resuscitation on her.

In one case, he probably actually killed the patient while someone else was in an adjacent room. Marie West, aged 81 was entertaining a friend, Marian Hadfield for tea one afternoon. Mrs. Hadfield had gone upstairs to the bathroom when Shipman arrived. She came back downstairs to hear Mrs. West having a conversation with him and did not want to interfere, so she waited in the kitchen. The conversation seemed to come to a stop and the silence lasted a while before Shipman entered the kitchen. He registered surprise when he saw Mrs. Hadfield but quickly recovered his composure and told her that Mrs. West had suddenly suffered a stroke while they were talking and he had briefly gone out to his car and returned to look for her son.

Shipman most likely killed using diamorphine, a chemically derived, more potent form of morphine – perhaps better known by its street name, heroin. Diamorphine is more commonly prescribed than morphine in the United Kingdom on account of its being more potent and faster acting. It very rapidly changes into morphine once it hits the brain so apart from a rush of euphoria caused by by-products of that process their action is indistinguishable.

Morphine, like all opiates acts by binding to certain sites in the brain and blocking the perception of pain so its primary use is in treating extreme pain from physical trauma, chronic conditions and terminal illness. It also has the effect of opening up arteries and easing blood flow, so it's also commonly administered to people suffering a heart attack (known medically as a myocardial infarction).

When administered into a vein, 40 milligrams of morphine and 20 of diamorphine are lethal in a healthy adult who does not regularly use them and hasn't built up a tolerance. In as little as one minute after injection the person's breathing stops and within five minutes they die from the lack of oxygen delivery to the brain. If nothing else it is a peaceful death, and Shipman's victims were often found in attitudes that resembled a deep sleep.

Shipman would acquire diamorphine using a method he had grown familiar with a long time ago – faking prescriptions and not maintaining a meticulous register of drugs administered. He would prescribe large quantities of diamorphine for terminally ill patients, sometimes after learning of their deaths, and then fail to bring the surplus in for destruction after they passed away. On one occasion he obtained

12,000mg of the drug in the name of a recently deceased patient, enough to kill at least 360 people. In a few cases he actually prescribed diamorphine for patients that he had killed.

All of the women whose cases were brought to the court had been fit and healthy in their old age, with no known serious long-term medical issues. The causes of death Shipman would put down were almost never consistent with any previous problems known by the relatives of the deceased. The most common one was a heart attack, such as in the case of Winfred Mellor, who was aged 71 when he killed her. Despite her advanced age Mrs. Mellor had been very active and in fact had taken a two-hour hill walk just a couple of weeks before her death. Another cause he stated was stroke, as he did with Marie West.

The situation of the deceased's bodies was not consistent with these causes of death at all. A person suffering a heart attack experiences a great deal of pain and can be expected to struggle, possibly attempting to get up and get help and ending up falling on the floor. A stroke is also not a particularly easy way to go – the sufferer notices that something is wrong.

Another two causes he listed on some deaths were pneumonia, as in the case of Joan Melia, aged 73, and Betty Adams, 77; and cancer as he did with Maureen Ward, 57. Neither of these two causes ever comes without a period of very obvious illness. Pneumonia also leaves easily identified traces in the lungs of the deceased but none were found during the post-mortem examinations.

In one case he named diabetes as the cause, and in several, such as that of Kathleen Grundy he listed "old age". Old age has a very specific definition as a cause of death – it is the simultaneous failure of multiple organs over a long period of time due to their natural degeneration as a person gets on in years. The only reason the term is allowed to be so vague is that the exact organ which has finally given out would be impossible to point out. Death of old age is a progressive process that can occur over a period of years during which the person is typically bedridden and needs round the clock care. None of the patients whose deaths he ascribed to it had been experiencing a noticeable decline.

The picture painted by the prosecution of Shipman was one of a cold, manipulative and calculating charmer who projected a front of kind gentility to get close to his patients, but once he was "through" with them, having gotten whatever he wanted from their deaths allowed the mask to drop and let his true, callous self come through. According to Detective Sergeant Philip Reade who came in on a routine visit after the death of Ivy Lomas, aged 63, Shipman laughed and called Mrs. Lomas a "nuisance". She had been something of a hypochondriac and he joked that he should have had a seat permanently reserved for her in his waiting room. He had left Mrs. Lomas dead in a hospital bed and gone on to attend to three other patients before she was discovered.

Another way in which his contempt for those who were left behind showed itself was the charade he would put on when the body of the deceased was discovered. The process of ascertaining that a person has died is very rigorous, composed of several steps and takes some time. The first step is to feel for a pulse — first at the wrist and then at the carotid artery on the neck. The doctor is supposed to spend about thirty seconds at each point, loosening any clothing at the neck if necessary. The doctor should then observe the chest wall for another thirty seconds for any sign that the patient (they remain a "patient" until death is actually declared and only become the deceased after that) is breathing, again loosening or removing clothing if necessary. They should also listen for breathing with a stethoscope for a further thirty seconds.

The next step would be to shine a bright light into the patient's eyes to check for any reaction in their pupils. The pupils become permanently dilated after death. The doctor would then use an ophthalmoscope to examine the blood vessels in the patient's eyes — once circulation stops the blood in them breaks up into short, alternating lengths, a phenomenon known as "cattle trucking". The final step is to forcibly flex the end of the patient's finger in order to elicit pain. If the patient were only in a very deep state of unconsciousness this would still cause them to flinch through the action of a reflex. Only then could the patient be declared dead.

Depending on the circumstances of the death some of these steps could be omitted, but it should be expected that at least most of them be performed. Shipman never did a single one of them, sometimes even declaring death without even coming close to or touching the body. What he typically did can only be described as theatrics and "movie medicine", playing on the expectations and preconceptions the family of the deceased would probably have gained from popular entertainment. When informing Mariah Hadfield of Marie West's death, all he did was open her eye and state to Mrs. Hadfield, "see – there's no life there". He would also briefly touch the patient's wrist and declare he could find no pulse.

On the occasion of Betty Adams' death, this lack of thoroughness almost came back to bite him. Bill Catlow, her long-time dancing partner let himself into her house to find Shipman in her living room. Shipman told him Mrs. Adams was very ill and that he had called an ambulance. After his usual cursory examination he declared her dead, but Mr. Catlow felt her wrist himself and told Shipman he could feel a pulse. Shipman dismissed this and told him it was his own pulse he was feeling and then went on to call to cancel the ambulance. This was only Mr. Catlow's testimony of things as he remembered them but it's quite likely Shipman had declared a patient dead while she was still alive.

The supposed call he made to the ambulance service was itself a part of his charade – he would claim to have called an ambulance, or would sometimes apparently make the call in the presence of friends or family of his victims. In some cases, like that of Mrs. Adams, he would claim to have already made the call and then would call again to cancel the ambulance after declaring the patient dead, other times he would make the supposed call, perform his "checks" while still on the call and then tell the ambulance service not to bother dispatching as the patient was already dead.

When call records were examined for the trial it was revealed that no calls had ever been made – it was all an elaborate act on Shipman's part. He could never have been as fast and loose with his examinations if he had actually been on the phone with an ambulance service – they would have called him out on it.

Shipman exhibited a lack of tact and sensitivity with the family and friends of the deceased not at all in keeping with what one would expect from a caring medical practitioner in the presence of the so recently bereaved. He was brusque with them in several cases, once stating that he "had the living to take care of". He would also make family members of the deceased feel guilty for not being aware of the deceased's pre-existing medical conditions, such as in the case of Pamela Hillier, aged 68, whose daughter he shamed for not having spent more time with her "sick" mother.

The medical conditions that "explained" the deaths of his victims were, of course, mostly fabrications. In the cases of a few patients, such as Mrs. Hillier and Maureen Ward, there really were conditions that could have contributed to their deaths, but their severity was nowhere near enough to be satisfactory. Mrs. Hillier, whom he put down as having a stroke, had a history of high blood pressure but, according to the testimony of a medical expert, it was such a minuscule problem that she was not at any higher risk of stroke than the general population. Mrs. Ward had had some spats with breast and skin cancer but was in the clear, and had been for a while.

For several others, Shipman was found to have inserted backdated entries into his medical records computer system that backed up his stated cause of death. He would date the entries sometimes as far as two years back, but the system kept track of the date that an entry was actually made, and so Shipman was caught out in this particular fabrication. One such case was that of Mrs. Grundy – on the day of her death he made an entry stating that she had come to him on the June 27th 1997 feeling tired and depressed, and he made a note with that entry stating "old?", apparently to corroborate his diagnosis of old age as her cause of death.

Mrs. Grundy's death is the one that set everything crashing down for Shipman, and it had an important place in the prosecution's case. Of particular interest was the supposed new will and the irregularities found in it. The forensic document investigator's testimony was submitted along with those of the two patients of Shipman's who had allegedly witnessed the will and of the law firm that received the will.

The two witnesses were Paul Spencer and Claire Hutchinson. Both had been in Shipman's waiting room when he asked them to witness a document in the presence of both Shipman and Mrs. Grundy. He did not tell them what the document, which already had Mrs. Grundy's signature on it was – Mr. Spencer was under the impression that it was a medical form of some kind, but Mrs. Hutchinson claimed she saw the words "last will and testament" on it. When shown the will, Mr. Spencer said the signature on it was not his and Mrs. Hutchinson said she could not be sure, though her address on it was incorrect.

Shipman had sometime before that told Mrs. Grundy of a supposed research program into old age that he recommended she take part in. There were supposedly some documents she had to sign – he probably got her signature for the purpose of copying it that way. This is probably also the ruse he used to get Mr. Spencer's and Mrs. Hutchinson's signatures.

The new will was delivered to the law firm Hamilton Ward just two scant hours before Mrs. Grundy's death. The solicitor who received the will, Brian Burgess expressed his surprise at receiving the will to the court – no one at the firm had ever dealt with or even heard of Kathleen Grundy.

Mrs. Grundy's signature on the will was definitely a forgery – and a bad one at that. The document was almost certainly typed on the typewriter found in Shipman's surgery and a fingerprint was recovered from it that turned out to belong to Shipman. Mrs. Grundy's fingerprints were nowhere on the document.

The closest anyone ever got to hearing a confession or admission of guilt was a district nurse Shipman talked to round about the time that Mrs.

Grundy's body was being exhumed. He joked that he should have had Mrs. Grundy cremated, stating himself the reasoning we deduced about his reasons for doing so earlier: "you can't exhume ashes".

The Defence's arguments

The word "defence" as applied in the criminal justice system can sometimes be misleading, conjuring an image of solicitors with loose morals and shark-like instincts who will twist the truth for the ends of a client they know is guilty. This dark image is not entirely deserved – the role that criminal defence plays in the justice system is absolutely vital and necessary for it to run both fairly and efficiently. The job of the defence is to present their client's side of events on a level that is equal to that of the representatives of their accusers, and to possibly be the one person who is on their side in a room full of people who are impartial at best but are most likely hostile.

The defence can only work with what their client tells them – if they admit guilt, the defence then work within that paradigm and try to get the least severe punitive measures on their client as possible. If they profess innocence, they must work with that in turn no matter how overwhelming the prosecution's arguments and evidence seem to be.

Since Shipman was maintaining his innocence, his counsel had to do their best to tear down the narrative built by the prosecution and build up the one most favourable to their client, using the information he supplied to them himself. As you can guess after reading the prosecution's case, boy did they have their work cut out for them.

The prosecution's case rested most heavily on the toxicology reports, and the defence consequently began by assaulting this aspect first. Forensic toxicology was at that time still very much a new-born science, and its methods were still being refined and perfected. There was not much in the way of precedents and hard data to build a whole lot of justifiable assumptions onto. Ms. Julie Evans the forensic toxicologist who performed the tests on the exhumed bodies herself said that she was "breaking new ground" in "novel scientific territory" when she began working on the case.

Not much detail was known about how chemical substances are altered and transformed after death, nor were the full effects decomposition has on the process understood. Whether or not all bodies experienced the same rates of alteration was a particular sticking point: the levels of morphine found in the bodies were consistent with those that had been known in the past to be present in the bodies of people who had died of overdose, but if the exhumed bodies had retained more morphine that would have thrown the entire analysis off. This really could have been a strong possibility – the bodies these old, morphine-naïve ladies were being compared to were those of long-time addicts with very high tolerances for the drug which might have broken it down faster and more completely after death.

The circumstances surrounding the death, ambient temperatures it had experienced from death to burial and beyond, the presence of other substances in the body – the effects of all of these were simply not fully known.

Shipman's appearance at patients' homes on the days of their deaths was explained as simple statistics coupled with sheer coincidence: we saw in the previous chapter how Shipman had long had a reputation for being an especially caring and proactive doctor, visiting his patients far more often than his colleagues. According to the defence, the assertion that he did this to get close enough to his patients to kill them was cynical and unwarranted. It was a freak phenomenon of random chance that he should have visited so many patients on the day of their death, but the scenario was not entirely implausible.

The irregularities with Shipman's prescription of diamorphine, his failure to destroy excess stocks and his possession of large quantities of it could simply be explained by the fact that he was a doctor and access to drugs comes part and parcel with that job, but he was not only that: he was a human being with a regular human mind sometimes prone to error and forgetfulness. In testimony to the court, he called his over-prescription of the drug a "bad habit" and that when he had delivered enough to a patient who needed it he would squirt the excess down the drain. The drugs that were not destroyed were not spared for the purpose of stockpiling – it was simple forgetfulness and procrastination on his part.

A lot of the causes of death he attributed his patients' demise to were because of a variation of the same factor: Shipman was not omniscient, he made the best guesses he could in the circumstances and he may have been wrong a few times. For a couple of the deaths the defence presented alternate scenarios that would explain the presence of morphine in the patients' systems. Bianka Pomfret, who passed at age 49 had had a history of psychiatric problems – she had manic depression. It was submitted as plausible that Ms. Pomfret had committed suicide by overdose.

For Mrs. Grundy, they took to Shipman's own testimony and several more notes he kept in his daybook. According to him, Mrs. Grundy had exhibited abnormally contracted pupils during one visit to his office, and Shipman had made a note questioning whether she was a drug user. On the day of her death, Shipman said, he had left her alive and well after his visit to her home and that she must have accidentally overdosed while trying to get high after he left. No drugs or drug paraphernalia of any kind were found in Mrs. Grundy's home.

The fact that Shipman had made backdated entries into his medical records computer was not disputed, but what they did throw doubt upon was the supposition that this had been done for nefarious purposes. It had simply been done to interject data that made sense in light of the patients' deaths that Shipman did not see as relevant at the time.

The defence presented Shipman's account maintaining that the second will was genuine. Shipman maintained that he had been approached by

Mrs. Grundy to have him witness a document. He said that he suspected she wanted to leave a modest sum of a few hundred pounds for his practice's patients' fund, which was used to buy equipment. He claimed to have actually joked with her about it being a large sum, saying he wouldn't sign off on her leaving him her entire estate.

He also claimed, and was backed up by his receptionist, that he had lent Mrs. Grundy the typewriter in question. The fingerprint that was found on the will was of him pushing it towards Mrs. Grundy.

The final ditch attempt by the defence was to attack the assertion the prosecution made way back at the beginning that Shipman had killed for his own personal pleasure, pointing out the flaws of making that conclusion. Establishing a motive is a particularly important consideration when a jury is deciding whether to convict and no one had really been able to seriously do that. The prosecution's presentation of this aspect in such a throwaway manner really begins to look more and more like a bad idea.

Sometimes, though, the rest of the case is just too strong, the evidence just too overwhelming. Shipman's case was just such a case – his defence had done the best they could with the raw material provided to them by Shipman himself but it was not enough to convince the jury. Shipman was found guilty on all counts and, on January 31st 2000 was sentenced to fifteen life sentences for the murders and, as a tiny bit of gilding on the lily, four years for the forgery of Mrs. Kathleen Grundy's purported will. The sentences were commuted to a single "whole life" sentence, the equivalent of life imprisonment without the possibility of parole.

On February 11th 2000, Shipman was officially struck off the General Medical Council's register.

CHAPTER 3 – THE SHIPMAN INQUIRY: UNCOVERING THE FULL EXTENT OF HIS CRIMES

Shipman was behind bars and, with the exception of just one, could and would take lives no more. It was immediately obvious, however, that what had been revealed during the trial was just the tip of the iceberg. The murders examined had gone back just over a year from the time of his arrest, and if that rate was extrapolated backwards the total number could have been astronomical indeed.

On February 1st 2000, the very day after Shipman's conviction, the Secretary of State for Health announced the commissioning of an inquiry to be chaired by Lord Laming of Tewin – the Laming Inquiry. The inquiry began the work of gathering information, but once it was discovered that it was a private inquiry and neither the evidence gathered or conclusions reached would be made available to the public or even the families of Shipman's victims, an outcry was raised.

The families of Shipman's known and suspected victims had organized into the Tameside Families Support Group and they made petitions to the Secretary of State. Many of them had grieved their family thinking they had died naturally, but the revelations of the trial had reopened old wounds and thrown on them the salt of uncertainty. They had a right to know if the deaths they were grieving anew had been deliberate or if they had been natural as claimed.

The public also had a right to know the full extent of his crimes – the entire nation and the world were reeling from the very idea of a murderous doctor and there was a need to understand how it had all been allowed to happen. Tragedies like this could be one-off but there is nothing new under the sun –unchecked, something similar could happen again. The public needed to know that whatever oversights had occurred were plugged so that they could rest easy in the knowledge that they or their loved ones wouldn't fall victim to their own doctor.

The Secretary of State initially maintained his position but after the Support Group and nine media organizations initiated legal proceedings decided to reconsider. On the 21st of September 2000, he announced that a public inquiry would be held. The Shipman Inquiry was officially set up on January 31st 2001, a year to the day after Shipman's conviction, and was headed by Dame Janet Smith.

The terms of the inquiry were fourfold: to determine the full extent of Shipman's unlawful activities, to figure out what actions and shortcomings by the authorities, individuals and procedures that should have stopped Shipman's activities allowed him to go on, to assess the performance of the procedures for monitoring medical professionals and the use of controlled drugs and, finally, to recommend what steps should be taken to better safeguard patients in the future.

The inquiry had a monumental task ahead of it: a total of 888 cases were investigated – 887 deaths and one incident involving a still-living person. Of these, 394 cases were immediately closed as they had no connection with Shipman, while 493 were thoroughly examined and received written verdicts, as did the one involving a living person. 2,311 police statements were examined from all of Shipman's contact with the law over the years and a further 1,378 were taken from anyone who could have helped give a more complete picture of the circumstances of the deaths. Statements were also taken from those who had worked with Shipman throughout his career. It would have been taken far too much time to hear testimony for all 493 deaths, so in the end a representative number of 179 testimonies relating to 65 of the deaths were heard.

A whole slew of documents were also considered, including coroner's reports, cremation forms, practice records and medical records. Due to the procedure of destroying medical records, few paper records remained from Shipman's time at the Donneybrook practice, though the introduction of the computer system in 1989 meant that those from then on did survive. Shipman had also taken advantage of a statute that allowed general practitioners to take possession of copies of their deceased patients' records after three years – these were found randomly stored at his house during the police raid instigated by the investigation into Mrs. Grundy's death. The inquiry also gained access to other documents that could shed light on the deaths, even including phone records and personal diary entries. In total, over 37,000 pages of documents were scanned into the image database that was used to distribute them to the investigation team.

Several media organizations attempted to gain the rights to broadcast the public proceedings of the inquiry. There was still a huge amount of public interest in the Shipman affair, and it was put forward that it was an extension of the public's right to know the full extent of what had happened for them to be able to watch proceedings unfold. CNN was one of the organizations that made the request, and actually asserted that it was a legal right by invoking Article 10 of the European Convention on Human Rights, which enshrines the right to freedom of information.

The Tameside Families Support Group and several other organizations representing those who would be testifying during the inquiry opposed this, particularly the broadcasting of the first phase, in which the families and close acquaintances of Shipman's victims would be testifying. The process of recalling such painful memories would put them in a good deal of distress, and they could also conceivably be reluctant to give evidence if they would be subjected to public exposure. Dame Smith agreed with this and, with the view that sensitivity for those close to the deceased trumped the right to publicity barred Phase One from being broadcast. However, she did agree to the broadcast of Phase Two, in which expert witnesses would be giving their testimony.

The entire inquiry was all the same still thoroughly documented and disseminated. There were cameras and screens within the Council Chamber at the Manchester Town Hall, where the hearings were held, as well as facilities for representatives of the media to use. The proceedings were immediately transcribed and transmitted to computers in the town hall and inquiry offices and within hours of a day's hearings would be posted up on the inquiry website, as were the scanned images of pertinent documents. The website itself was fully public and had received 15,000 unique visitors by April 2002.

It was also decided that the citizens of Hyde, who had a direct stake in the matter should have a right to watch proceedings as they unfolded, so a feed was piped live over CCTV to the Hyde Public Library where community members could view the footage and images of relevant documents as they came up.

Harold Shipman himself refused to participate in the inquiry. There could have been a measure that might have compelled him to cooperate – issuing him a summons, with the threat of additional prison time if he refused. But Shipman was already serving a whole life sentence and that threat would have held no fear for him. There was nothing anyone could do to get him to testify.

There had been a clamour to have Shipman tried for any further murders that were uncovered, but it was decided soon after the conclusion of his trial that this would serve no purpose. First of all, the publicity that the trial had attracted would make any further trial impossible to conduct fairly, and second was the issue of the whole life sentence once again – what would be the point of trying him if he could not have any extra prison time imposed on him?

Primrose Shipman appeared to have had some involvement in two of the deaths. She, on the other hand, was a free woman who could have her freedom taken away from her and so was issued with a summons. There was, however, the condition that whatever evidence she presented could not be used against herself or her husband. She cooperated fully with the inquiry, going so far as to volunteer some documents that wound up revealing more damning information about her husband.

Shipman's victims year by year

The inquiry thoroughly investigated each of the 493 deaths that had some connection to Shipman. In the end, 215 of these were confirmed by the testimony given and evidence examined to almost certainly have been murdered by Shipman.

The earliest confirmed killing happened during Shipman's time at the Abraham Ormerod Medical Centre in Todmorden. Eva Lyons was 70 years of age and had been suffering from terminal cancer. On March 17th 1975, Shipman visited her late at night at her home. Mrs. Lyons' husband was with them in the room when he gave her an injection in the back of the hand and Shipman sat in conversation with him until she died a few minutes later. Mrs. Lyons' husband suspected that Shipman had "helped her on her way" and confided this suspicion to their daughter. It's likely that Shipman had administered an opiate drug to her and remained with her afterwards so that he could be present to make sure she died.

Mrs. Lyons was the only person Shipman is confirmed to have killed at Todmorden out of 21 deaths examined from that period. There were a further six that raised some suspicion but could not be confidently confirmed. Five of the suspicious deaths were of patients who were terminally ill, and three of those were very gravely ill and could have been expected to pass away naturally at any moment. The circumstances around them do not shed enough light to make a conclusive decision.

One death was of a reasonably healthy woman, though – Edith Roberts, aged 67 was found dead in her bed four days after Mrs. Lyons' death. Mrs. Roberts had had a history of diabetes and chest pain. She was found lying peacefully in bed with a book beside her. Shipman certified her death as having been due to a heart attack – inconsistent with her attitude upon death as we have already seen. Her door was locked, however – from the inside, meaning she would have been able to see Shipman out and lock up before going to bed. It may be that Shipman departed from his usual routine and administered the drug that killed her via the intramuscular route, which takes longer to take effect hence giving her time to see him out. Without more evidence her death could not be confirmed outright as a murder.

The publicity around Shipman's trial brought out a testimony that may have pointed out Shipman's first attempt to kill. This was the one case involving a living person – Mrs. (later Professor) Elaine Oswald. On

August 21st 1974, Mrs. Oswald made an appointment with Shipman complaining about pain in her left side. Shipman diagnosed her with a kidney stone, prescribed her with Diconal (a mild opiate) and sent her home with the promise of a visit to take some blood samples. This was likely just a ploy to get alone with her – the appropriate test for a kidney stone is a urine sample.

Shipman arrived in the late morning after Mrs. Oswald had taken the Diconal and was feeling drowsy. Whether he actually took a blood sample or not is unknown, but while he was there Mrs. Oswald went into respiratory arrest. Shipman performed CPR on her and called an ambulance. It was suspected that she had overdosed on the Diconal but it seems clear in hindsight that Shipman had injected her with an opiate, possibly pethidine. His attempting to revive her does make it seem that his intention wasn't to kill her, however.

Mrs. Oswald was 25, way outside his usual victim's age range, which brings up a possible motive: perhaps Shipman wanted to involve Mrs. Oswald in his pethidine use, maybe with a view of coercing her into entering a sexual relationship with him. He may have miscalculated the amount of pethidine he gave her or failed to take the Diconal she had taken into account and was legitimately startled when she stopped breathing. This salacious allegation is no fabrication of the author of this book to add spice to the narrative – it was seriously considered and proposed by Dame Smith herself in the inquiry reports.

The gulf until the next killing is quite wide, caused in no small part by Shipman's pethidine woes and the break in his career they caused. He did not have access to controlled drugs or any meaningful opportunity to kill during his years at the Newton Aycliffe Health Centre.

The possibility arose again once he began working at the Donneybrook practice. Shipman still did, however, have the spectre of his drug convictions looming behind him. He had, after all, made a promise not to carry controlled drugs again and he was probably under heavy scrutiny from his new partners. As a result he would have avoided signing off on drug orders and making prescriptions, at least not early on before he gained his partners' trust. In the first ten months of his time at Donneybrook there are no confirmed killings, though there was one death that raised some suspicion.

His first confirmed murder at Donneybrook – that of Sarah Marsland, 86 on August 7th 1978 – was the first to conform to what could perversely be called Shipman's "style" – an unannounced visit to an elderly but still active female patient's home, Shipman himself present during the death (found in this case, interestingly, by another one of his future victims – Mrs. Marsland's daughter Irene Chapman) and certifying the death as having been due to a heart attack. He claimed to have tried to resuscitate her, and yet she was on her bed – correct procedure for attempting resuscitation is to move the patient onto a hard surface such as the floor.

There are three more confirmed killings from 1978 and a further four suspicious deaths. It's likely that Shipman acquired the drugs he used for these first murders from two patients who had died of cancer in late July of that year.

The early part of 1979 had three suspicious deaths, and the next confirmed killing was that of Alice Gorton, aged 76. Shipman went to Mrs. Gorton's home around lunchtime on August 9th, supposedly to deliver some topical medication for chronic psoriasis she suffered from. There was an interesting break to Shipman's routine in this case – after presumably administering the opiate to Mrs. Gorton, Shipman went to the house of her daughter Mrs. O'Neill who lived nearby, visited every day and had in fact been with Mrs. Gorton earlier in the day. He told Mrs. O'Neill that her mother was very ill and she should follow him immediately. When she arrived, she found Shipman in the living room. He went on to tell her that there would be no need for a post-mortem – a needlessly obfuscatory way of informing her of her mother's death that was a habit of Shipman's.

He was obviously under the impression that he had done his dirty deed to completion, so you can imagine his surprise when they heard a loud groan coming from the bedroom – Mrs. Gorton was still alive. She had quite probably not been breathing for a while, however – which is what would have convinced Shipman she was dead – and had likely suffered irreversible brain damage. Shipman was saved the prospect of her waking up to tell her version of the story when she died 24 hours later.

This incident probably startled Shipman, but obviously not enough – his next victim was Jack Shelmerdine, a 77 year-old sufferer of chronic bronchitis with a failing heart. Shipman was called out to Mr. Shelmerdine's home on November 28th 1979 to attend to an episode of breathlessness. He gave him an injection of intramuscular diamorphine, after which he lapsed into unconsciousness and died 30 hours later.

Mr. Shelmerdine's son lodged a complaint with the Regional Health Authority about the lack of geriatric care his father had received in his final hours. Shipman was required to make a statement over the matter and admitted to giving Mr. Shelmerdine 10mg of diamorphine, though it was likely that he administered more with the intention of ending his life.

The fact that he had miscalculated his dosages on two consecutive occasions, coupled with the complaint which, although it was not directly against him could have led to a post-mortem exam probably tipped the balance of fear in Shipman. The whole of 1980 went by with no confirmed killings and only one suspicious death.

On April 18th 1981 Shipman killed Mrs. May Slater, aged 84. For this killing he employed a strategy for gaining time alone with a patient in a nursing home while simultaneously shielding himself from the family of the deceased that he would use intermittently over the coming years: he distracted Doreen Laithwaite the warden of Mrs. Slater's nursing home by making her meet with the family while he performed the deed (he normally would have had to be accompanied by her during his visit) and then had Mrs. Laithwaite inform them of Mrs. Slater's death.

There was one more confirmed killing in 1981 that followed his usual method, but there were also four suspicious deaths, including two that heavily deviated from Shipman's normal method. Ann Coulthard and Elsie Scott were both quite old – Mrs. Coulthard was 75, Miss Scott 86. Mrs. Coulthard had previously suffered two strokes, while Miss Scott's state of health couldn't be determined at the time of the inquiry, though she was in a nursing home. Shipman may have used Largactil, a non-opiate (and hence not controlled) analgesic instead of his usual diamorphine.

Shipman gave Mrs. Coulthard an injection of a substance that was probably Largactil on the 7th of September which caused her to become very sleepy and she was heavily sedated for the whole of the next night and day. He told her family the next day that she would probably die before the day was out and indeed she did about an hour after he gave her another injection that evening. It is known that he gave Miss Scott an injection of Largactil on October 6th – a dose of about 100mg. The recommended dose for elderly patients is 25mg. Miss Scott was heavily sedated until she died 18 hours later.

A state of heavy sedation is heavily discouraged in older patients – it massively increases the chance of developing bronchopneumonia, an inflammation of the lining of the lungs which was confirmed as the cause of Miss Scott's death. It seems likely that Shipman intended for both ladies to die, though the uncertainty of this method and the large time-gap between administration of the drug and death are not in keeping with his usual method.

It seems possible that the change in the drug of choice was because of a shortage of easy-to-obtain supplies of opiates, and there were only four suspicious deaths through the whole of 1982. The next confirmed killing was of Percy Ward, a 90 year-old sufferer of duodenal cancer on January 4th 1983. The killing of Moira Fox on June 28th of that year was his first killing of a healthy, independent victim since August 1981.

Mrs. Fox was also the first confirmed case of what would become another recurring theme in his killings: visiting the patient on the pretext of taking a blood sample. This would have served two purposes: first of all he would have used the act of supposedly drawing blood to distract the patient to what he was actually doing – patients typically aren't all that aware of what their doctor is up to when having blood taken, and Shipman could actually have asked the patient to look away during the procedure. The second purpose would be to explain away the needle mark in the patient's skin if it was ever inspected. This habit probably did lessen the risk of his being found out somewhat but he didn't use it all the time and got away with his crimes just fine on those occasions.

The first victim of 1984 was Dorothy Tucker, only 51 but severely overweight to the point of needing a wheelchair to move around and also suffering from varicose ulcers on her legs. In a call to her cousin Mrs. Mary Bennett on January 7th, she explained that she had not been feeling well and called in Dr. Shipman, who had given her an injection. She expressed a desire to sleep and after that conversation was not heard from alive again.

With Mrs. Bennett, Shipman introduced yet another element to his repertoire: leaving the furnace set on high so that the room the deceased was found in was unusually hot. A hot room causes rigor mortis to set in faster but reduces the rate at which the body's temperature drops – both factors used to estimate time of death. This could have served to throw off any estimate enough to land it safely outside the time of his visit. Another possible reason that may have come into play later on is one we've contemplated with respect to forensic toxicology. It could be that Shipman intended to speed up the breakdown of opiates in the deceased's body so that if a toxicology analysis were made it would detect lower levels and reduce suspicion of overdose.

On February 8th Shipman would kill Gladys Roberts, a 78 year-old widow who lived alone. He had been called in to look at a leg ulcer Mrs. Roberts suffered from and killed her while they were alone. This would be the first time Shipman would claim to have made an emergency phone call – Mrs. Roberts' daughter Enid called her house to check on her after she failed to make a call she had promised to. Shipman answered the phone and told Enid that he had been on the phone with the hospital when Mrs. Roberts died, according to him of a pulmonary embolism (an air bubble from the lungs entering the bloodstream). Because it happened so long ago it's impossible to know for certain whether or not Shipman actually did call the hospital, but judging from later incidents we can almost be sure he didn't.

There would be four more confirmed murders and four suspicious deaths in 1984.

New Year's Day 1985 saw two suspicious deaths, but his first confirmed victim of the year died the next day and would be the youngest known at that stage of the inquiry – Peter Lewis, aged 41 was in the last stages of terminal cancer. Shipman probably sped up his demise and also used the opportunity to avail himself of Mr. Lewis' remaining stocks of opiates. The rest of the year saw ten more killings, including one day on which two occurred – those of Thomas Moult and Mildred Robinson on the 26th of June. There was also one further suspicious death that year.

Judging by the relative scarcity of Shipman's contact with terminal cancer patients in 1985 it seems likely that this was the first year that he began obtaining opiates by issuing false prescriptions in the names of patients who neither needed nor ever received them. He had been working at the practice for close to eight years by that point and had by that time gained enough trust and confidence to pull this off without detection.

Shipman killed eight in 1986, including two women who lived on the same street and had the same two housekeepers. Miss Mona White was killed on September 15th and Mrs. Mary Tomlin on October 7th. In both cases the two housekeepers, Elizabeth Shawcross and Dorothy Foley witnessed Shipman's proximity to the deaths but if they found this unusual they did not voice their opinions. 1986 also witnessed two suspicious deaths.

The first case in which GP records survived was also the first case of 1987. On March 30th Shipman killed Frank Halliday, 76, who was generally poorly. The records state that Mr. Halliday had been complaining of chest pains for two days before that, but that is highly unlikely as if it were true his sister, who was at the time on holiday in Scotland would have been told and likely returned immediately. This was also the first of several recorded cases where Shipman wrote down that he administered opiates to the patient to ease chest pain – always either 10mg of morphine (as in this case) or the equivalent 5mg of diamorphine – probably to cover for the presence of the lethal dose he had given them.

The usual procedure in legitimate examples of this practice is to slowly inject the drug into the patient's vein and observe their reaction – morphine acts almost immediately so its effect is pretty much in real-time. The doctor administering it should then write down exactly how much of the drug was administered and over what length of time – something Shipman never did in these cases.

There were seven more killings and one suspicious death that year.

Shipman's oldest victim was killed within a cluster of four murders in a single week and two in one day. On February 15th 1988, Shipman took the life of Ann Cooper, aged 93, who was still active and self-dependent despite her age. There had been two murders in that year before this mini-spree, but afterwards followed a gap of seven months. It's likely that this sudden uptick in deaths had not gone unnoticed, probably drawing the comment of one of Shipman's partners, so he chose to lay low for a while. All the same, five more murders followed after the break as he regained his confidence.

Twelve patients saw their end at Shipman's hands in 1989. The first patient he killed at his practice's premises was 81 year-old Mary Hamer. Mrs. Hamer was in good health and visited Shipman's practice on March 8th of that year for an issue the nature of which never became known to the inquiry. Shipman saw two or three patients after killing her, and before informing the practice's receptionist that she had died. He told her family that she had come in complaining of chest pains and put her death down to a heart attack. The last killing of the year was that of Joseph Wilcockson on November 6th, who was found dead but still warm by the district nurse who had come to dress a varicose ulcer he suffered from. The district's nurse involvement set tongues wagging at the practice and this probably gave Shipman another scare.

Shipman wouldn't kill for another ten months and would only kill two people in 1990 and none at all in 1991. It's likely that he had started to see the difficulty of maintaining a high kill rate while working in a shared practice and tried not to raise any more suspicion while he was preparing to move out on his own.

All told, Shipman killed 171 while a partner at the Abraham Ormerod Medical Centre, and a further 30 deaths occurred under suspicious circumstances but could not be confirmed.

When we look at Shipman's killing patterns, it is immediately obvious that he left the Donneybrook practice with the intention of gaining the freedom to take his killing up to the next level. There was only one suspicious death in the part of 1992 during which he was practicing independently within Donneybrook house. Within six weeks of establishing his own practice he would kill: on October 7th, 72 year-old Monica Sparks would hold the dubious honour of being his first victim at the Market Street surgery.

In the early part of 1993, Shipman would establish a grisly rhythm: killing a patient and then filling out a prescription for 30mg diamorphine in their name on the day of their death or shortly afterwards to replace the ampoule he had used in killing them. One intended victim during this period may have had a very narrow escape: on August 31st, the step-daughters of Mrs. Mary Smith walked in on Shipman leaning over her while she was unconscious. She slept very deeply until the next morning. It seems likely that they may have interrupted him while he was administering diamorphine to her and caused him to stop before he had delivered a fatal dose.

The scare that came from this close call probably caused Shipman to take a break until December 1993. Fearing having a pattern identified, he never prescribed 30mg diamorphine again, instead switching exclusively to appropriating the leftover stocks of his deceased terminal cancer patients. The amounts he got in this way are stupendous – the first time he did this he may have obtained 3,000mg, enough to kill up to a hundred and fifty people. The three patients he killed that December brought the year's death toll to 16, already a record year. It wasn't even close to the highest count he would reach.

Shipman killed three times in early 1994 before having another serious scare on February the 18th. Mrs. Renate Overton was suffering an asthma attack when Shipman was called to her home to see her. Mrs. Overton's daughter was with her at the time and went upstairs when the attack had been dealt with. Shipman called the daughter down saying her mother had collapsed and gone into cardiac arrest. The daughter called an ambulance while Shipman attempted to resuscitate her. He must either have been more successful than he intended or the ambulance may have arrived too soon for his liking, but the ambulance crew managed to revive her, although she had suffered massive brain damage. Mrs. Overton remained in a coma until she died 14 months later on April 21st 1995.

Mrs. Overton's death prompted some questions from the coroner for Greater South Manchester. Shipman's retelling of the event left out any mention of diamorphine, but if medical records had been checked his administering it to her would have been uncovered. Due to a law that was then in effect that stated that a person could not be tried of murder due to actions undertaken more than a year and a day past, Shipman would not have faced murder charges for her death but could still have been charged with attempted murder. Unfortunately, the coroner did not order an inquest into the matter.

His failure to kill Mrs. Overton led to another gulf of three months. Mary Smith, who he had previously failed to kill, would unfortunately turn out to only have received a stay of execution. She had developed lung cancer over the intervening period. Shipman acquired 1000mg of diamorphine in her name before killing her with part of that stock on May 17th.

The number of confirmed killings in 1994 was 11, with two suspicious deaths that year as well.

Including Mrs. Overton's, 1995 saw 30 killings confirmed, and one suspicious death. The first killing for which Shipman was tried and convicted, that of Maria West (whose friend was waiting in the kitchen while Shipman killed her), happened on March 6th that year.

There were another 30 killings in 1996, one of which, that of Irene Turner would form part of the murder trial. In one, that of 72 year-old Edith Brady in his surgery he would perform a new piece of charade when ascertaining death. When he called in his practice manager to witness the death, he touched the back of Mrs. Brady's neck, claiming to be checking for brainstem activity and stating that there was "nothing there". John Grenville, the medical expert consulting for the inquiry would call this "pure charlatanism".

1997 was Shipman's most prolific year, seeing 37 confirmed murders, of which seven were part of the trial that brought him down. 1998, the final year in which he was free to perform his dark deeds saw 18 murders, of which six received convictions. The perception and reality of Shipman's nature finally begin to come together at this point.

New revelations from Pontrefract General Infirmary

When the inquiry started on its investigations, the possibility that Shipman could have started killing while he was a house officer at Pontrefract General Infirmary was considered, but was quite quickly discounted. This proved to have been a hasty move, however: as events unfolded more people would come out of the woodwork to reveal more details of the picture.

One such person was Sandra Whitehead, who had been a student nurse at PGI in 1971 when Shipman was serving there. On February 4th 2004, Mrs. Whitehead testified that her time at PGI was fraught with bad memories because of the high number of patient deaths she experienced there. When she realized that she had worked with Shipman at PGI, she instantly made the connection – The high death rate must have been connected with Shipman.

Dame Smith decided the inquiry must look deeper into the matter. Death certificates and cremation forms from PGI were thoroughly assessed to ascertain a connection with Shipman before relatives of the deceased were contacted – they had already taken the solace of the first verdict but would have unnecessarily had the uncertainty return anew if they had been questioned despite the death having no connection. Grounds for some suspicion were found in 133 deaths, and of those the inquiry managed to make contact with the relatives of 117. Statements were then taken from them.

Statements were also taken from several more of Shipman's colleagues from PGI which revealed a great deal of information as well as some additional details about Shipman's character and reputation while at PGI. The character revelations were largely in keeping with what we already know of Shipman: generally a loner, occasionally insufferable and superior, popular with patients but also, interestingly, formed very strong friendships and made uniformly positive impressions on a couple of his colleagues.

There was a plentiful supply of pethidine at the facility as it was the most commonly used opiate analgesic at the time. There were also plenty of other non-controlled drugs Shipman could have used to kill, including Largactil (which, as we have already seen, he would later use in several suspected killings) and potassium chloride, which is used to replace potassium ions lost through excessive urination but in large enough doses can cause cardiac arrest – this lethal quality actually makes it a drug of choice in legal executions. It is also all but untraceable in toxicology.

Shipman certified more deaths in the evening – from 6pm to midnight – than should be statistically possible. The period covers a quarter of the day, so you would expect it to contain a quarter of deaths – and yet 54% of Shipman's certified deaths occurred during this period. It appears to have been a time of opportunity for Shipman as he seems to have had more time alone with patients during that period.

Shipman's colleagues also reported in him an overconfidence verging on recklessness, particularly when he was administering drugs to patients. He would sometimes administer drugs far too quickly and in amounts far too excessive. It could be that in these cases he was experimenting with the effects of large doses of certain drugs and not actively trying to kill.

All told, there were 14 deaths that held mild suspicions of having been intentionally caused by Shipman, four that were found to be seriously suspicious and three that were confirmed as unlawful killings. A further three were found to probably have been caused by extreme recklessness on Shipman's part. All were very ill in some way or in dire medical emergencies.

Six cremation Form B's for young children were filled out by Shipman.

Of these, he reported that he was alone with the child at the time of their death in three cases. This should not be possible: a child in the final stages of illness typically receives a great deal of attention from parents, relatives and nurses and is unlikely to be alone at the moment of death.

Still, when most of them were examined most were found to have been natural. Only one raised suspicion: Shipman's youngest possible victim was Susie Garfitt – just four years old, she had cerebral palsy and was quadriplegic. Susie's mother Ann was at her daughter's bedside when Shipman told her that the prognosis was not good and Susie could only be kept alive with continuous medical intervention – and an implication that doing so would be "unkind". Mrs. Garfitt told Shipman to "be kind" to Susie, though she was not implying that he should quicken her death. All the same, when she went to get a cup of tea she returned ten minutes later to find Susie dead. Without knowledge of if Shipman had any drugs with him that could have precipitated Susie's death it's impossible to know for certain, but the proximity of the conversation to her death makes it seem extremely likely.

The confirmed killings from PGI brought Shipman's total up to 218. The actual numbers are probably much higher – assuming half the "suspicious" deaths were murdered by Shipman, this brings a conservative estimate of 238. Shipman's cellmate reported that he had in private confessed to 508 murders, but this seems way too unlikely and, being the testimony of a convict, is probably not to be trusted.

HAROLD SHIPMAN

81

CHAPTER 4 – SHIPMAN'S MOTIVES AND MOTIVATION

Even the lowest estimate of 218 lives taken over a career of thirty years is an appalling figure, and it leaves all empathetic human beings with the question: why? We struggle to comprehend the reasoning when a single person is killed, but 218? As much as we can try to understand it, an instinctive grasp of the state of mind necessary eludes us.

For many cases, we at least have the reasoning spelled out to us in the killer's own words. For Shipman, we never will – no matter how overwhelming the evidence, he never uttered a word of confession to anyone credible through to the very end – at least not to anyone who's talking. He never once publicly boasted of the lives he's taken At least this factor allows us to discount one explanation with certainty: he didn't do it for the acclaim. As arrogant and self-important as Shipman was, he never intended for his crimes to be found out, let alone become famous because of them.

For everything else we'll have to guess, and try our best to reconstruct from the facts what the probable combination of factors that drove him was.

Clues from his childhood

As stated way back in the beginning, Shipman's childhood definitely had a huge influence on his future. The most obvious factor was his mother Vera's death and his proximity to it. Watching a loved one slowly succumb to a terminal illness is a difficult thing to experience, and it is impossible to come out of it unchanged in some way. The effect of the experience on Freddy Shipman's young mind must have been devastating and the change it wrought was a dark one.

It's possible that Shipman seeing his mother's doctor near-miraculously take away her pain gave him the drive to emulate that, but ended up going too far – it may have transmuted into the urge to take away the pain completely by delivering his patients into the complete painlessness of death. This explanation is corroborated by deaths much like that of little Susie Garfitt – terminal patients whose remaining lives would be short and either filled with pain or a featureless cloud of heavy sedation. The fact that all of his victims at PGI and most of his early ones in Todmorden were terminal patients possibly shows that this was his biggest motivation earlier on, but the greater profusion of healthy victims later on show that if it was it fell away as time went on.

Whether or not a victim was on their last legs and not going to last much longer does not excuse Shipman's hastening of their death. There may be some debate to be had over whether it would be acceptable if the patient was going to live the rest of their lives in either a stupor or unbearable pain, or their relatives consented, but the rest of his crimes definitely make Shipman a villain and not a saviour.

The alternative explanation for Shipman's targeting of terminally ill patients may be that their deaths are just easier to explain and he never did have anyone's best interests at heart. As time went on and he continued to stretch the boundaries without being caught, he may simply have gained more confidence and widened his victim pool.

The whole affair may simply have awakened unquenchable morbid fascinations in Shipman. He may simply have been infatuated with death, or perhaps with opiates as shown by his addiction to pethidine.

The fact that most of Shipman's victims were elderly women may be significant in that it may point back again to mother issues. He may have held some resentment over his mother's death that manifested itself into a desire to kill as many older women as he could. The gender aspect may not be as important as that of age, however: women tend to live longer lives than men and become a larger portion of the population as age rises. It could be that women were simply a more plentiful resource.

Clues from his character

Shipman's character as reported by those close to him may shed some light on his reasoning. The sense of superiority he acquired from his mother definitely followed him throughout his career, even manifesting itself in a casual disdain during his interviews with the police after he was caught. It may have directly influenced his actions as well. Shipman may have seen himself as capable of making the decision over whether it was time for a patient to "go". Many of his conversations with victims' friends and family support this postulate – he would often tell them that the death had happened at "the right time" or "for the best".

Following from this may have been a sense of frugality in Shipman: the United Kingdom has a single-payer tax-funded healthcare system – the National Health Service. All citizens are entitled to receive care through it free of upfront charge. Shipman may have intended to remove the drain on the service by terminally ill patients who were going to die soon as well as older patients who would become more and more demanding on the system without contributing into it as time went on.

In a few cases, he probably killed to get rid of patients who were heavily demanding on his time due to hypochondria such as Eileen Cox, who he killed in 1984, or psychological issues, such as Joan Harding, killed in 1994. He occasionally went as far as to actually call certain patients a nuisance, as he did Ivy Lomas.

The elaborate theatre he put on for victims' friends and family in the immediate aftermath of a killing also may have stemmed from his sense of superiority: he might have taken some pleasure in so thoroughly fooling them, and he may have enjoyed being in the limelight for that brief period.

He was also a control freak, and that desire for control may have grown into a desire to control the ultimate, of life and death.

Psychological issues

Shipman's addiction to pethidine tells us that he may have had an addictive personality, prone to unhealthy fixation on certain things. Confessions from serial killers often detail how they simply couldn't stop. The feeling they got from ending a life kept them coming back again and again. If indeed he did have an addiction to dealing death, Shipman may have had some control over it as shown by the breaks he took whenever he experienced a scare. All the same, he would invariably return after the hiatus, which does give the theory some credence.

Shipman did once ask a home care nurse whether or not she felt a 'buzz' when she found a patient dead – implying that he probably felt it himself.

The depression he professed when he was caught out for abusing pethidine may have been genuine. Sufferers often express a distance and perceived dislike from their compatriots regardless of if the relationships are actually on good terms. If Shipman did suffer from a depressive disorder it may have contributed to his drive to kill.

Personal gain

A motive worth looking at whenever older folk are murdered is that of financial gain. The forged will that got Shipman caught might seem to point to this, but it has its own microcosm of details that throw some doubt on that – we will discuss it on its own. What would be more indicative of gain as a motive is if Shipman used a large number of deaths to accumulate wealth.

Shipman was alone in the deceased's house for the vast majority of his killings, raising the possibility that he could have stolen items in the process. In one case he was found studying a victim's display cabinet while she lay dead in another room. Perhaps trying to pick out the most valuable item to take? A few families did report jewellery or sums of money missing after a death.

Shipman would occasionally ask for a memento of the deceased. What this suggests is that he wanted trophies of his killings, pointing to some deep psychological motive.

Police seized a box containing some jewellery from Shipman's home. Some was found to belong to Mrs. Shipman and returned to her. Of the rest, only one – a platinum diamond ring – was positively identified by a family. The rest were auctioned off and the proceeds given to the Tameside Families Support Group.

Further clues from the Grundy affair

Shipman's forging of Kathleen Grundy's will was a new and unique development in Shipman's repertoire, and badly executed in a way that may shed more light into his state of mind. The surface explanation is that his greed had exploded to a whole new level and he wanted to increase his financial returns from killing.

It seems unlikely, however, that he planned to continue with this new element. It might be possible to get away with one forged will, but multiple ones – not so much. Even if he had gotten away with it, the drama that would surround the affair would have made it extremely difficult to continue killing – he would have been under much heavier scrutiny. It seems likely that Shipman was considering putting a stop to the killing – whether because he had grown tired of it or because the pressure from the investigation of earlier in 1998 had shown him how close he was to being found out.

The forgery was so terrible that it was immediately obvious that it was a forgery, and it seems incredible that Shipman would have expected it to work. This raises the possibility that he had become delusional and really did believe it to – his descent into incoherence during the first police interview seems to confirm this. It could also be that he had grown subconsciously tired of all the killing and the will was a way of forcing himself into a position where he could no longer do it even if he felt compelled to.

The death of Harold Shipman

The truth is probably a combination of all of the above factors, but as already said, we will never know from the horse's mouth. On January 13th 2004, the day before his 58th birthday, Harold Shipman was found dead in his cell. He had hung himself using his bedsheets. Since he left no suicide note we can't know for sure his reasons for killing himself, but we can make a few guesses.

If desiring to control life and death was part of Shipman's motivation, it could go towards explaining his suicide. In many cases where it is a motivator, once the killer has been backed into a corner or caught, the ability to exert that control over others is taken away from them and they often resort to the one life they do have some remaining control over: their own. Suicide may have been the final, crowning act of control for Shipman.

Another two likely explanations involve his wife Primrose: the first is one he told a prison officer: if he died after 60, Primrose would not be eligible to receive an NHS pension and lump sum. If he died before then, however, she would receive them.

Primrose had unflinchingly stood beside Shipman and believed wholeheartedly in his innocence – her handing in of documents that damaged his interest's points to a genuine belief and not the actions of someone who wanted to defend a person they believed to be guilty. But in the end, that faith may have begun to crack: she reportedly sent him a letter not long before he killed himself asking him to "tell [her] everything no matter what". Losing his one unfailing supporter may have caused him to crack.

Whatever his reasons were, Shipman's death brought up the question of how we should react to the death of a monster. Some thought it cause for celebration, with tabloids running celebratory headlines to break the news.

For the actual families of those who had been killed, however, there was no celebration. He had died without ever confessing or giving an explanation for why their family members had been killed. For those whose family member's death had merely been branded "suspicious", they would never even know if they had been killed or not, always in a perpetual state of not knowing.

CONCLUSION – FINDING AND FIXING THE OVERSIGHTS THAT ALLOWED SHIPMAN TO KILL

A near-continuous campaign of murder like Shipman's does not happen without massive exploitable gaps and blind spots in important systems and people's reasoning. Those gaps were almost large enough for activities of Shipman's magnitude, which means that it's possible many smaller-scale sprees also fell through. In a way, this particular killing spree may have a positive aspect, in that in being too large to fall through completely it prompted the closing of those gaps so that the smaller cases could no longer slip through.

It was the introduction of a completely new and obvious element that got Shipman caught – it seems likely that if it had not been for the forged will he would have gone on killing for who knows how long. The factors are all there in the story as it's been presented so far, but it is necessary to analyse each of them in turn so that we can get a better understanding of them and prevent something similar from happening in the future.

A part of the reason Shipman managed to be so prolific were the cracks in the system of monitoring and certifying deaths through which he slipped. There simply was no concrete system for monitoring each doctor's patient death rate, and "honour systems" like the ones which were in play are vulnerable to abuse by people like Shipman with no honour at all. If there had been a system that automatically initiated an inquiry into a doctor with too high a death rate, Shipman probably would not have made it beyond his house officer years at PGI without being detected. Those cracks were sealed, new systems of accountability put in place that made sure any anomalies were immediately investigated to make sure there was nothing nefarious causing it.

The death and cremation certification procedures were also woefully full of holes that were vulnerable to exploitation. At no point did the family of the deceased get an opportunity to look at any of the documents, allowing Shipman to invent causes of death and lingering illnesses out of whole cloth, as well as claim the presence of people who were never there. The Form C doctor was supposed to "carefully examine" the body to confirm that it had not suffered a sudden death, but the conditions were never ideal to do that. Many doctors saw Form C as just being a "rubber stamp" on Form B. The triple-check provided by Form F also failed similarly. The importance of cremation to Shipman's modus operandi prompted enough concern to warrant an over 600-page volume report from the inquiry with suggested corrections in the procedure, which were implemented.

The bungles made by Law Enforcement throughout the years of Shipman's murderous career would make a good bumbling caper comedy if only the rest of situation was not so tragic. The entirety of

Detective Inspector Smith's time on screen would warrant Yakety Sax playing in the background. Shipman's case certainly caused them to perk up and completely change the way they approach investigations.

There's a saying that if you want backstage access to any show or concert, you don't ever really need a pass. You only need a few things: a black turtleneck, work gloves, a coil of cable, a ladder and a determined look on your face. With that get-up, you can walk into any restricted area – even get legitimate staff to swipe you through locked doors with no questions asked. If you have the right look and attitude and exude enough confidence, people tend not to question you. The deepest root of Shipman's success lies in this principle – the way he presented himself is what allowed the rest of the systemic failures to fall in place for him and obscure his true purpose.

Most of the oversights on the part of people who should have realized something was off but just weren't able to connect the pieces are really not their fault. Shipman, like many, many other serial killers, was a consummate manipulator, capable of presenting a front that fooled thousands over the course of his career. The very qualities that endeared him to his patients and allowed him to get close enough to take their lives were the very same ones with which he pulled the wool over everyone's eyes.

The position of a doctor is naturally one in which we imbue a great deal of trust. By looking like the perfect, noblest example of that profession,

Shipman distracted even those who should have known better. His colleagues were probably well aware of the number disparity between their patient death figures and Shipman's, and they knew on an intellectual level that there was something wrong with them statistically. And yet their conscious minds just couldn't allow them to connect those facts with the possibility that Shipman could be using his position to commit murder. Even those who did not like him just had far too much trust and respect in his position to figure it out.

Others connected to the medical profession who should have realized something was wrong allowed themselves to be duped. During his first time being investigated over pethidine, Shipman was defended by pharmacy staff who had the figures of the amount he was acquiring right in front of them. In several cases, Shipman murdered multiple charges of some caregivers and still they didn't think to raise suspicion. Mortuary staff, Form C co-signing doctors, crematorium workers – all failed to notice the patterns. During the first time Shipman was being investigated for possibly killing his patients, Alan Massey of Frank Massey and Son, Funeral Directors went so far as to visit Shipman to tell him about what he saw as a ridiculous investigation.

A family member or friend of someone recently deceased is typically in a state of shock and grief upon learning about it. They can't be held responsible for failing to think clearly in that situation and Shipman would actually take advantage of that. The charade he put on for the deceased's families worked especially because of their grief and confusion. He would also use it to forestall the body receiving a post-mortem exam and also to press the family to destroy the evidence for him by having the body cremated.

Ultimately, no matter what systems are in place, those systems are run by people. If those people remain inattentive enough even the best-planned systems will fail. Shipman's crimes certainly awakened us all to the possibility of those we trust the most being the ones who are out to hurt us, and it remains to us to recognize the warning signs around us. It's not just those in the medical profession that are in a position of life and death over us. Whatever you do, always be ready to investigate anything that looks anomalous and raise alarm when it is due. You never know – lives may depend on it.

ABOUT THE AUTHOR

Ryan Green is an author and freelance writer in his late thirties. He lives in Devon, England with his wife, three children and two dogs. Outside of writing and spending time with his family, Ryan enjoys walking, reading and wind surfing.

Ryan is fascinated with History, Psychology, True Crime, Serial Killers and Organised Crime. In 2015, he finally started researching and writing his own work and at the end of the year he released his first book on Britain's most notorious serial killer - Harold Shipman.

His books are packed with facts, alternative considerations, and open mindedness. Ryan puts the reader in the perspective of those who lived and worked in proximity of his subjects.

Made in the USA
Middletown, DE
19 December 2016